The Caregiver Companion

Essentials for Family Caregiving

Edna Pittman-Rouce

To Tim and Demarion
You've taught me what unconditional love looks like.
I'm thankful God thought I could handle the assignment.

Table of Contents

INTRODUCTION

When life changes in an instant: A Mother's Journey into Caregiving

I never imagined that one day, in a single moment, life as I knew it would shatter. My son was three years old when a tragic accident changed everything. His daycare center forgot him in a hot van on a scorching August afternoon, and by the time they realized their mistake, the damage was done. My once energetic, curious little boy

—who had been feeding himself, running, playing, and learning—was suddenly left completely disabled.

In that instant, I became more than just his mother—I became his full- time caregiver. His life had changed forever and so had mine. The dreams I had for him—watching him grow, explore the world, and carve out his own path—were replaced by an overwhelming new reality. He would never progress as his siblings had. He would never regain his independence. Instead, he would rely on me for everything, for as long as I was alive.

When this journey began in 2007, I had no roadmap, no guidebook. I was thrown into a world of medical jargon, insurance battles, endless therapies, and surgeries. I went from celebrating his potty-training milestones to relearning how to care for him as if he were a newborn. He could no longer see, walk, or even hug me with his tiny hands. Every day was a lesson in survival—his and mine.

There were moments of exhaustion, frustration, and deep sorrow. Guilt weighed heavy, and happiness became something I measured in medical reports. But through it all, I learned. I learned how to navigate systems designed to be complicated. I learned to fight for my son's needs. I learned that caregiving isn't just about the person you care for—it's also about taking care of yourself. And I learned that I was not alone.

This handbook is for every caregiver who has ever felt lost, overwhelmed, or invisible. I don't claim to be an expert, but I do know the power of experience. If sharing my journey can help even one person feel less alone, then every struggle, every tear, and every small victory has been worth it. I hope this book gives you insight, strength, and the encouragement to keep going— because you are not alone in this journey.

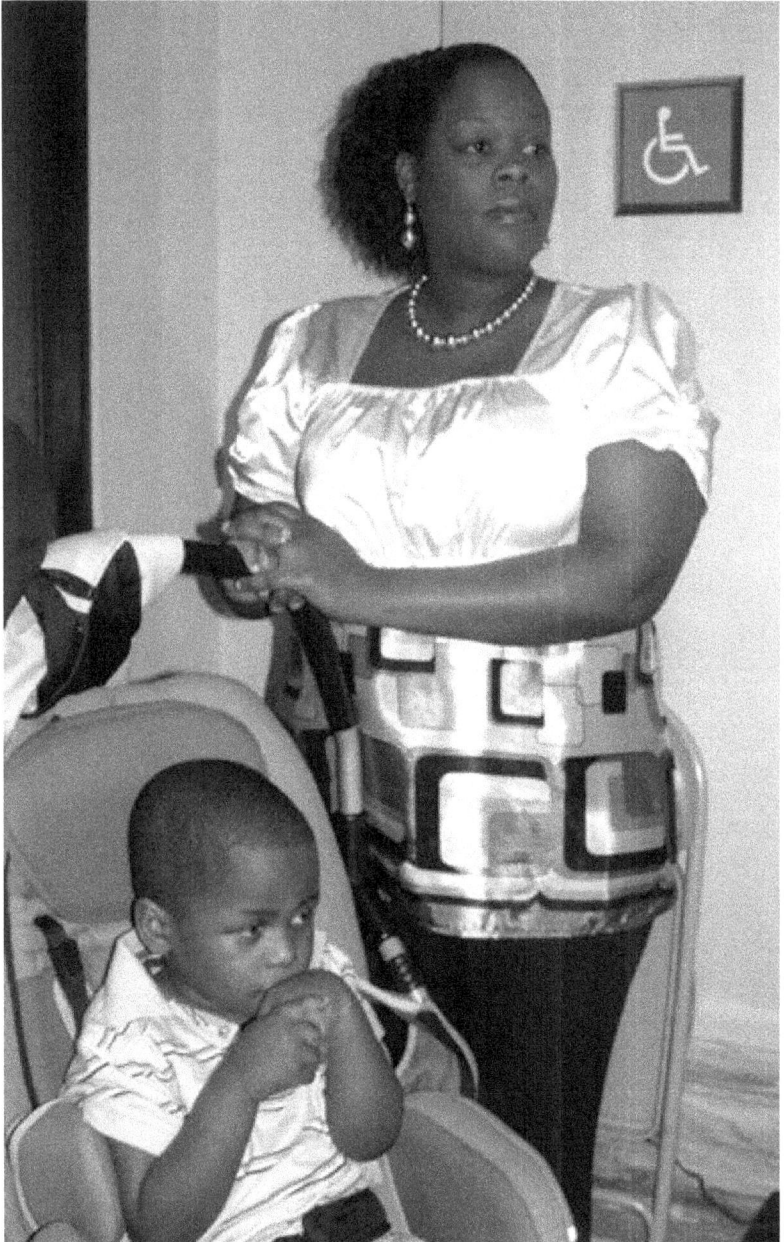

Edna with her son Demarion at the Oklahoma State Capitol pushing for Demarion's Law in 2008.

EMOTIONAL AND MENTAL WELL-BEING FOR CAREGIVERS

Managing stress, avoiding burnout, and maintaining a positive mindset are crucial for caregivers. Here are practical strategies to help:

1. **Recognizing the Signs of Stress & Burnout**

- Feeling overwhelmed, fatigued, or emotionally drained
- Experiencing frequent headaches, sleep disturbances, or mood swings   Losing interest in activities you once enjoyed
- Becoming easily irritated or resentful·

2. **Stress Management Techniques**

- Practice Deep Breathing & Mindfulness: Spend a few minutes each day focusing on deep breathing or guided meditation. Apps like Headspace or Calm can be helpful.
- Stay Active: Engage in light exercise like walking, yoga, or stretching to release tension.
- Take Breaks: Step away for short moments of rest, even if it's just a few minutes of quiet time.

- Journal Your Thoughts: Writing down your emotions can help process stress and provide clarity.
- Listen to Music or Audiobooks: Soothing sounds can reduce stress and uplift your mood.

3. Avoiding Burnout

- Set Realistic Expectations: Accept that you can't do everything. Prioritize tasks and delegate when possible.
- Ask for Help: Reach out to family, friends, or professional respite care for support.
- Join a Caregiver Support Group: Connecting with others who understand your journey can offer emotional relief and practical advice.
- Establish Boundaries: Learn to say "no" to additional responsibilities that overwhelm you.
- Take Care of Your Health: Eat nutritious meals, stay hydrated, and get enough sleep.

4. Maintaining a Positive Mindset

- Shift Your Perspective: Focus on what you can control rather than dwelling on frustrations.
- Celebrate Small Wins: Acknowledge the efforts you make daily, no matter how small.

- Practice Gratitude: Keep a gratitude journal, listing at least one positive thing each day.
- Stay Connected: Talk with friends and family to maintain a sense of normalcy.
- Engage in Activities You Enjoy: Read, garden, paint—anything that brings you joy and relaxation.

As a caregiver, there are many things beyond your control, but focusing on what you can manage makes a significant difference. By implementing these small yet impactful strategies, you can stay strong, motivated, and prepared to handle the challenges that come with caregiving. I never promised this road would be easy— but I'm here to tell you, it *is* possible. It took me years to realize that small, intentional steps—taken whenever and however I could—would profoundly shape not only my well-being, but also how I showed up in the lives of those I cared for. When I finally gave myself permission to focus on the little things that helped me breathe, reset, and regain perspective, the days began to feel less overwhelming, and the burden less heavy. In those quiet shifts, I found strength. And in that strength, I rediscovered myself.

BALANCING CAREGIVING WITH WORK AND PERSONAL LIFE

Balancing caregiving with work and personal life is one of the greatest challenges caregivers face. The emotional, physical, and mental demands can be overwhelming, but with the right strategies, it's possible to manage these responsibilities while maintaining your own well-being. Here are some practical approaches:

1.   Mastering Time Management

- Prioritize Tasks: Use a planner or digital calendar to structure your day.
- Identify essential tasks and break them into manageable steps.
- Create Routines: Establishing predictable routines helps streamline daily caregiving, work, and personal commitments.
- Use Time Blocks: Set specific time slots for caregiving duties, work, self- care, and leisure. This prevents tasks from overlapping and causing unnecessary stress.
- Embrace Flexibility: Things won't always go as planned. Build in buffer time for unexpected situations.

2.   Setting Boundaries

- Communicate Your Limits: Be clear with your employer, family, and friends about your availability and the support you need.
- Say No Without Guilt: You can't do everything. Prioritize what truly matters and decline commitments that drain your energy.
- Separate Work and Caregiving: If working from home, designate a workspace and set clear working hours to minimize distractions.
- Enforce Personal Time: Schedule time for yourself—whether it's a hobby, a short walk, or quiet time to recharge.

3.   Maintaining Relationships

- Stay Connected: Even short check-ins with friends and family via calls or messages can help maintain social bonds.
- Seek   Support: Join caregiving groups or talk with others   who understand your situation. You are not alone.
- Plan Quality Time: Schedule regular date nights, family outings, or solo breaks to nurture important relationships.
- Ask for Help: Don't hesitate to delegate tasks to other family members, friends, or professional caregivers when possible.

4.   Self-Care is Non-Negotiable

- Prioritize Health: Eat well, stay hydrated, and get enough rest. Your well-being directly impacts your ability to care for others.
- Find Stress Relievers: Exercise, meditation, journaling, or engaging in hobbies can help reduce stress and prevent burnout.
- Seek Professional Help if Needed: Therapy or counseling can provide guidance on managing stress and emotions.

Balancing caregiving with work and personal life isn't easy, but with strategic planning, support, and self-care, it is possible to maintain a fulfilling life while providing the best care for your loved one.

On my personal journey, I've discovered a few lifelines—quiet practices that saved me in ways I never expected. Journaling was the most natural starting point. I've always loved to write, and pouring my thoughts onto paper gave me a safe place to speak freely—without judgment, without fear. It became my sanctuary, a place where I could tell the truth, fall apart, and find clarity.

Therapy, on the other hand, wasn't something I imagined for myself—not at first. I believed prayer would be enough, and for a long time, I leaned on that faith alone. But therapy kept being suggested, gently and persistently, until one day, I said yes. I wish I had said yes sooner. It has been nothing short of lifechanging. Even when I couldn't make it into a physical office, online therapy met me where I was— whether in the chaos of caregiving or on the road. Carving out one hour, no matter what, became sacred— a gamechanger for my mental health.

Through therapy, I was introduced to meditation. And now, when the noise of caregiving feels too loud or the days stretch too thin, I find space to simply *be*. To breathe. To return to myself.

What's worked for me may not be what works for you. But I hope, with all my heart, that you find something— anything—that grounds you, heals you, and reminds you that *you* matter, too.

NAVIGATING HEALTHCARE AND FINANCIAL PLANNING

Navigating healthcare and financial planning as a caregiver can be overwhelming, but having the right strategies and resources can make a big difference. Here are practical ways caregivers can effectively manage these areas:

1. **Understand the Medical System**

- Learn the Diagnosis: Understand the condition your loved one is facing—symptoms, progression, treatment options.
- Build a Healthcare Team: Establish relationships with doctors, nurses, therapists, and case managers.
- Keep a Medical Binder: Track appointments, medications, test results, and provider contact info.
- Use Patient Portals: Many health systems offer online access to records, lab results, prescriptions, and messaging.

2. **Master Insurance and Benefits**

- Know the Coverage: Understand what Medicare, Medicaid, private insurance, or VA benefits cover—and don't cover.
- Request Case Management: Some insurance plans offer case managers to help navigate care coordination.
- Check for Long-Term Care Insurance: See if your loved one has a policy and learn what services it includes.
- Review Explanation of Benefits (EOBs): Understand what's been paid and what might be your responsibility.

3. **Legal Planning and Protection**

- Advance Directives: Help your loved one complete documents like a living will and durable power of attorney.
- Guardianship/Conservatorship: Explore if legal authority is needed for decision-making.
- Review Estate Planning Documents: Wills, trusts, and beneficiary designations should be up to date.
- Consult an Elder Law Attorney: Especially important for Medicaid planning, asset protection, and long-term care.

4. **Financial Planning and Budgeting**

- Track All Expenses: Maintain a caregiving budget that includes medical, transportation, and household costs.
- Explore Financial Aid:
  Medicaid (state-dependent for long-term care)
  Supplemental Security Income (SSI)
- State and local aging services
- Nonprofits and disease-specific grants
- Tax Deductions/Credits: Some caregiving expenses may qualify for deductions (e.g., medical expenses, Dependent Care Credit).
- Speak with a Financial Advisor: Preferably one experienced with elder care or special needs planning.

5. **Use Community and Government Resources**

- Area Agencies on Aging (AAA): Local organizations that connect caregivers to services and supports.
- SHIP (State Health Insurance Assistance Program): Offers free help with Medicare questions.
- Veterans Affairs (VA): Offers healthcare, home care, and financial aid for qualifying veterans.

- Disease-specific Organizations: (e.g., Alzheimer's Association, American Cancer Society) offer guides, hotlines, and local support.

6. **Maintain Documentation**

- Keep records of:
Medical and financial decisions   Legal documents
Conversations with healthcare providers
Expenses and receipts for reimbursement or tax filing

7. **Plan for Emergencies**

- **Create a crisis plan including:**
1. Emergency contacts
2. Medication lists
3. Hospital preference
4. Legal documents in an accessible place

8. **Join a Caregiver Support Group**

- Learn from others navigating similar systems.
- Gain emotional support and discover tips for managing bureaucratic challenges.

NAVIGATING CAREGIVING WITH A SPECIAL NEEDS CHILD

My caregiving journey took an unexpected turn when Demarion turned three. Up until then, school had never crossed my mind. I was consumed with navigating the maze of medical diagnoses that followed his heatstroke—trying to understand, treat, and survive each one. School felt like a distant reality, something for other children, other families. We were in survival mode.

Then came the phone call that changed everything. It was someone from the school district. At first, I didn't understand why they were calling. But as she spoke, my heart began to shift. One of my daughter's teachers had visited us in the hospital after the accident. She saw the challenges ahead and, without hesitation, notified the special education department. She told them about my son, about the kind of support he would need—not someday, but *now*.

That's how I was introduced to Child Find. They quite literally *found* my son—saw him, acknowledged him, and opened the door to possibilities I hadn't dared to imagine. At just three years old, Demarion was enrolled in the school system. It felt like someone had pulled us from the shadows and said, "You're not alone in this."

Looking back, I believe that single act made all the difference. It wasn't just about academics. It was about hope. It reshaped how I saw his future—and mine.

Caring for my child marked the beginning of my caregiving journey. Almost immediately, I found myself navigating a whirlwind of responsibilities and information I never imagined I'd need to understand. Parents of children with special needs often face unique challenges—and fortunately, there are many resources available to support them across healthcare, education, legal rights, financial assistance, and emotional wellbeing.

Here's a breakdown of the main types of resources:

1. **Early Intervention Services**

   - IDEA Part C (Individuals with Disabilities Education Act): Provides services for children from birth to age 3, including speech, physical, and occupational therapy.
   - Child Find Programs: State-run programs that identify and evaluate children who may need early intervention.
   - Local School Districts: Often coordinate evaluations and Individualized Family Service Plans (IFSPs).

2.   **Educational Support**

- IEP (Individualized Education Program): A legal document outlining specialized educational services for children aged 3–21.
- 504 Plans: Accommodations in general education settings for children who don't qualify for an IEP but still need support.
- Parent Training and Information Centers (PTIs): Provide free guidance about special education rights and services.
- Special Education Advocates: Help parents navigate school systems and meetings.

3.   **Healthcare and Therapy Resources**

- Children's Hospitals and Specialty Clinics: Offer developmental evaluations, therapies, and care coordination.
- Therapy Services:
- Speech-Language Pathology   Occupational Therapy (OT)
- Physical Therapy (PT)
- Behavioral Therapy (ABA, CBT)
- Telehealth Services: Increasingly available for therapy and consultations.
- Developmental Pediatricians: Specialists who diagnose and coordinate treatment for developmental disorders.

4.   **Financial Assistance and Benefits**

- Supplemental Security Income (SSI): Monthly benefits for children with qualifying disabilities and limited family income.
- Medicaid Waivers: Cover home and community-based services not normally included in Medicaid.
- Children's Health Insurance Program (CHIP): Low-cost insurance for children in families that earn too much for Medicaid.
- ABLE Accounts: Tax-free savings accounts for disability-related expenses without affecting SSI/Medicaid eligibility.

5.   **Legal and Advocacy Support**

- Wrightslaw.com: Comprehensive site for legal information on special education.
- Disability Rights Organizations: Offer free legal help and advocacy (e.g., Disability Rights Education and Defense Fund).
- Special Needs Trusts: Protect assets for a child's future without affecting government benefit eligibility.
- Guardianship and Supported Decision-Making: Legal structures to help parents plan for long-term care and independence.

6.   **Respite and In-Home Support Services**

- State and Local Agencies: Often offer respite care to give parents a break.
- Home Health Aides / Personal Care Assistants: Can help with daily tasks or medical needs.
- Medicaid-funded Support Programs: Vary by state but may include in- home support, day programs, and caregiving stipends.

7. **Parent Support Networks and Communities**

- Parent-to-Parent USA: Matches parents with trained support peers.
- Facebook and Online Groups: Specific to conditions (e.g., Down syndrome, autism, cerebral palsy).
- Local Support Groups: Through hospitals, schools, or community centers.

8. **National Organizations**

- Autism Speaks
- National Down Syndrome Society   Cerebral Palsy Foundation
- The Arc
- Easterseals
- Family Voices These often provide toolkits, grants, webinars, and helplines.

9. **Planning for Adulthood**

- Transition Planning in IEPs (starts by age 14–16): Prepares for independent living, employment, and post-secondary education.
- Vocational Rehabilitation Services: Help teens and young adults with job training and employment.
- Postsecondary Education Options: Inclusive college programs for students with intellectual disabilities.
- Independent Living Centers: Support transition to adult services.

PARENT RESOURCE GUIDE FOR CHILDREN WITH SPECIAL NEEDS

Early Childhood (Birth to Age 5)

Key Focus Areas

1. *Early diagnosis and intervention*
2. *Building a care team*
3. *Legal and financial planning*

Resources

Early Intervention

- IDEA Part C Programs (State-run)
- Child Find Services
- Local School Districts (for IFSPs)

Medical & Therapy

- Developmental Pediatricians
- Speech/OT/PT Evaluations
- Children's Hospitals
- Early childhood mental health programs

Financial Support

- Medicaid / CHIP
- SSI (if income-eligible)
- Medicaid Waivers (state-specific)

Parent Support

- Parent to Parent USA
- Family Voices
- State Parent Training and Information Centers (PTIs)

Legal/Planning

- Special Needs Trust (via estate attorney)
- ABLE Accounts (savings without penalty)
- Durable Power of Attorney (future planning)

PARENT RESOURCE GUIDE FOR CHILDREN WITH SPECIAL NEEDS

School Years (Ages 5–18)

Key Focus Areas

1. *Education rights and accommodations*
2. *Behavior and learning supports*
3. *Inclusion and independence*

Resources

Education Support

- IEP (via IDEA)
- 504 Plans
- PTIs (Parent Training Centers) Wrightslaw.com (legal help)

Therapy & Services

- In-school OT/PT/Speech
- ABA therapy
- Behavioral Therapy (CBT, DBT)

Medical/Behavioral

- Pediatric Neurologists
- Child Psychologists
- School counselors and social workers

Financial Assistance

- Continued SSI eligibility
- Transportation support (if needed via IEP)
- Medicaid waivers for in-school or home care

Parent Communities

- Local and online support groups (condition-specific)
- Facebook Groups
- Nonprofits (Autism Speaks, NDSS, The Arc)

PARENT RESOURCE GUIDE FOR CHILDREN WITH SPECIAL NEEDS

Transition to Adulthood (Ages 14–21+)

Key Focus Areas

- Life skills and independence
- Vocational training and employment
- Legal and financial planning for adulthood

Resources

Education & Career

- Transition planning in IEP (starts at 14–16)
- Vocational Rehabilitation Services
- Inclusive college programs (e.g., Think College)

Life Skills

- Independent Living Centers (ILCs)
- Community-based training
- Special transition coaches

Legal Planning

- Guardianship or Supported Decision-Making
- SSI (adult eligibility)
- Special Needs Trust or ABLE account

Adult Services

- Medicaid adult waivers
- Group housing or supported living
- Day programs or employment services

Parent Support

- Advocacy groups (local, state & national)
- Local and national webinars on transition
- State developmental disability services offices

SPECIALIZED CAREGIVING

Specialized caregiving refers to the care and support provided to individuals with medical, developmental, or psychological conditions that demand targeted knowledge, customized routines, and skilled coordination. Unlike general caregiving, this type of care involves a deep understanding of specific health issues and the ability to navigate complex care systems.

I learned most of what I know about specialized caregiving while taking care of my late husband. His diagnosis required me to gain in-depth knowledge about the disease and learn how to accommodate him in daily living, treatment, and support.

What Does Specialized Caregiving Involve?

1. Condition-Specific Knowledge

Understanding the medical condition's symptoms, progression, and treatment options.

Keeping up with current research, therapies, and care strategies.

2. Tailored Daily Care

Adapting daily routines to accommodate sensory, mobility, dietary, or behavioral needs.

Using assistive technology or specialized medical equipment, such as ventilators, feeding tubes, or mobility aids.

3. Medical Collaboration

Working closely with a team of specialists, including neurologists, developmental pediatricians, and therapists.

Managing medication regimens, therapy schedules, and home health services.

4. Behavioral and Emotional Support

Implementing therapeutic approaches such as Applied Behavior Analysis (ABA), cognitive-behavioral therapy (CBT), or trauma-informed care.

Supporting emotional regulation and mental health through routines,

reassurance, and positive reinforcement.

5. Legal and Educational Advocacy

Navigating legal protections such as IEPs (Individualized Education Programs) and 504 Plans in school settings.

Advocating for accommodations, disability rights, and long-term planning options like guardianship or supported decision-making.

6. Emergency Preparedness

Developing individualized emergency plans for medical crises, behavioral outbursts, or natural disasters.

Training in first aid, CPR, and condition-specific emergency responses (e.g., seizure protocol).

Examples of Specialized Caregiving Needs

- Autism Spectrum Disorder (ASD)
- Alzheimer's and Other Dementias
- Cerebral Palsy
- Muscular Dystrophy
- Spinal Cord Injuries
- Traumatic Brain Injury (TBI)
- Genetic Disorders (e.g., Rett Syndrome, Fragile X Syndrome)
- Severe Mental Health Disorders

Why Specialized Caregiving Matters

I've come to understand that specialized caregiving isn't just about meeting medical needs—it's about preserving dignity, reducing chaos, and creating stability in an already unpredictable journey. When my husband was first diagnosed with diabetes and later experienced kidney failure, I thought I just needed to learn a few new routines. What I didn't realize was that I was stepping into a whole new world—one where small details could mean the difference between life and crisis.

I had never considered how something as simple as a power outage could become a life-threatening event. But suddenly, the machines in our home—machines that helped keep him stable, breathing, and safe—depended on electricity I had always taken for granted.

That's when I learned that being proactive wasn't just helpful—it was vital. Knowing the emergency protocols, registering for priority restoration with the utility company, having back-up plans—these things mattered more than I ever imagined.

I also discovered that *home health care* is not just for the patient. It's for the caregiver, too. When your hands are full, and your heart is heavy, having trained professionals to share the load can make all the difference. It's not a weakness to ask for help—it's wisdom.

Being aware of the unique needs of your loved one doesn't just ease their suffering. It reduces your stress, restores some control, and allows you to care from a place of preparedness rather than panic. Specialized caregiving taught me to think ahead, advocate fiercely, and breathe deeper—because peace of mind, even in the hardest moments, is worth fighting for.

CAREGIVER SELF-CARE AND PERSONAL GROWTH

You Matter Also: Caring for Yourself While Caring for Others

I've shared a lot of practical advice and resources to help you navigate caregiving. But now, I want to shift the focus — to the heart of it all... you.

Caregiving often asks us to pour so much of ourselves into others that we forget who we are outside of that role. It's easy to lose pieces of your identity while caring for someone you love.

This next chapter is for you. It's an invitation to pause, reflect, and reconnect with yourself. My hope is to encourage you to prioritize your own health, nurture your passions, and honor your goals — even in the midst of caregiving.

Because you matter, also.

In case no one has told you lately — or in case you just need to hear it again: Caring for yourself is not selfish. It's essential.

The Forgotten Person in the Room

There's a quiet epidemic happening in the world of caregiving — burnout. Exhaustion. Emotional depletion.

And far too often, the caregiver — you — becomes the forgotten person in the room.

We've been sold a harmful myth: that self-sacrifice equals love. That the more we neglect ourselves, the more devoted we must be. But that's not love — that's burnout waiting to happen.

I want to give you permission — full, heartfelt permission — to reset. To pause. To check in with yourself. It's time to name what caregiver guilt really is and face it with truth and compassion.

You deserve care too — starting right here, right now.

What are the causes of Caregiver Guilt?

Unrealistic expectations:

Caregivers often place incredibly high expectations on themselves — and when they can't meet them all (because no one can), guilt quickly follows.

Burnout:

The constant demands of caregiving can leave you physically and emotionally drained — and that exhaustion often opens the door for guilt to sneak in.

Loss of control:

Caregivers often carry the heavy weight of wanting to fix what cannot be fixed. It's hard to watch someone you love decline — and even harder when you feel powerless to stop it or unsure if you're making all the right decisions.

Conflict with other responsibilities:

Caregivers are often pulled in many directions — juggling caregiving responsibilities alongside work, family, and everyday life. It's a constant balancing act, and when there's never enough time or energy to go around, feelings of guilt and even resentment can quietly build.

Social stigma:

Society often paints a picture of what it means to be a "good" caregiver — selfless, tireless, always available. But those unrealistic expectations can create guilt when caregivers feel like they're falling short of an impossible standard. The truth is, there's no perfect way to be a caregiver — only the best you can do with love, honesty, and grace.

The Weight of Caregiver Guilt

Carrying around constant guilt doesn't just affect your thoughts — it can take a real toll on your body, mind, and relationships. Over time, unaddressed caregiver guilt can lead to:

- Increased stress and anxiety

- Feelings of sadness or depression
- Trouble sleeping or constant fatigue
- Physical symptoms like headaches, tension, or illness
- Strained relationships with family, friends, or even the person you're caring for

Guilt drains energy you need for healing, connection, and self-care. That's why it's so important to name it, challenge it, and release it — for your health and well-being.

How Can I Break Free from Caregiver Guilt?

Breaking caregiver guilt isn't about never feeling guilty again — it's about learning to recognize it, understand it, and release it with compassion.

1. *Name the Guilt Out Loud*

Guilt loves to hide in silence. Start by saying it or writing it:

"I feel guilty because..."

Bringing it into the light takes away its power.

2. *Challenge Unrealistic Expectations*

Ask yourself:

"Would I expect this from someone else in my situation?"

If not — you've likely picked up an unrealistic standard. Give yourself permission to release it.

3. *Replace Guilt with Truth*

Guilt says: "I'm not doing enough."

Truth says: "I'm doing the best I can with love and care." Create your own truth statements to speak over your guilt.

4. *Create Healthy Boundaries*

Sometimes guilt shows up when you say "no" or set a limit. Remember: boundaries aren't selfish — they're necessary for survival and sustainability in caregiving.

5. *Make Time for You — Without Apology*

Guilt might whisper that taking time for yourself is wrong. But rest, joy, and connection refill your energy and make you a stronger caregiver.

Start small — 5 minutes of quiet, a short walk, a creative hobby, or a call with a friend.

6. *Ask for Support*

Talk to a trusted friend, a counselor, a faith leader, or a caregiver support group. Guilt loses its grip when you're not carrying it alone.

7.   *Forgive Yourself Daily*

You will have hard days. You will feel stretched thin. You will make mistakes. You are still worthy of love, care, and compassion — especially from yourself.

Practical Self-Care for Real Life

Self-care doesn't have to be big to be powerful.

Micro Self-Care Practices:

- 5-minute resets: deep breathing, stretching, gratitude journaling, stepping outside.
- Mind-body practices.
- Creating pause pockets.

Set Boundaries:

"I'm not available right now, but I will be at 3 PM." "Let me check in with myself and get back to you."

 Delegate and ask for help without guilt.

Find timesaving options (online resources for shopping, making appointments, meal-prepping, ask for help)

Reclaim Your Identity

Caregiving often puts dreams on pause — but growth is still possible, even in small ways.

Find You Again:

Writing a "Personal Growth Bucket List" — tiny things that light you up.   Journaling:

"What did I love before caregiving?"

"Who am I becoming through this experience?"

Learning: free online classes, podcasts, or books in bite-size chunks.   Creative Expression — art, music, writing, photography.

You are a caregiver — but not only a caregiver.

Personal Growth Inventory:

- Who was I before caregiving?
- What brings me joy now?
- What small dreams can I honor today?

TOOLS FOR CAREGIVERS

1.   Daily Care Tasks

- Monitor and assist with personal hygiene (bathing, dressing, grooming)
- Help with mobility (walking, transferring from bed to chair, etc.)
- Prepare and provide meals/snacks according to dietary needs
- Track fluid intake and nutrition
- Ensure medications are taken on time and in the correct dosage
- Check for any new symptoms or changes in health

- 2.   Medical & Health Management
  - Maintain a list of medications (names, dosages, and purposes)
  - Keep a record of doctor's appointments and follow-ups
  - Track vital signs if needed (blood pressure, glucose levels, etc.)
  - Prepare questions for healthcare providers before appointments
  - Keep emergency contacts and medical history readily accessible
  - Refill prescriptions and stock up on necessary medical supplies

3.   Emotional & Social Well-Being

- Schedule time for social interaction (phone calls, visits, outings)
- Engage in enjoyable activities (music, reading, puzzles, etc.)
- Monitor for signs of depression, anxiety, or distress
- Encourage independence and decision-making when possible
- Offer emotional support and patience

4. Home Safety & Comfort
- Ensure the home is free from tripping hazards (loose rugs, clutter)
- Check that mobility aids (walkers, wheelchairs, grab bars) are in place
- Adjust lighting for better visibility, especially at night
- Set up an emergency alert system if needed (wearable alert button, phone access)
- Keep essential supplies within easy reach

5. Caregiver Self-Care Checklist
- Take breaks and schedule time for yourself
- Eat well and stay hydrated
- Get enough sleep and manage stress levels
- Reach out for support (family, friends, support groups)
- Know when to ask for help or consider respite care

Caring for a loved one comes with many responsibilities, and having a checklist can help you stay organized and ensure their well-being. The following are key areas to consider:

Daily Care Tasks

Assisting with hygiene, mobility, meals, hydration, and medication management is crucial. Keep an eye out for any changes in health or symptoms.

Medical & Health Management

Maintain a detailed record of medications, doctor's appointments, and vital signs. Prepare questions for healthcare providers and ensure prescriptions are up to date.

Emotional & Social Well-Being

Encourage social interaction, engage in enjoyable activities, and monitor emotional health. Supporting independence and offering patience are essential.

Home Safety & Comfort

Ensure the home is safe with mobility aids, proper lighting, and an emergency alert system. Keep essential supplies within easy reach to enhance comfort and safety.

Caregiver Self-Care

Caregiving is one of the most profound acts of love and sacrifice. But as noble as it is, caregiving can take a silent toll—emotionally, physically, and spiritually. Many caregivers become so immersed in tending to their loved one's needs that they neglect their own health, happiness, and personal fulfillment. The result? Burnout, resentment, fatigue, and even illness.

Self-care is not selfish. In fact, it's one of the most selfless things a caregiver can do. When you care for yourself, you refill your cup and show up as the best version of yourself—not just for your loved one, but for everyone around you. You cannot pour from an empty vessel.

Why Self-Care Matters in Caregiving

Improves your health: Chronic stress from caregiving can weaken the immune system, increase blood pressure, and contribute to anxiety or depression. Self-care helps reduce these effects and restores balance.

Prevents burnout: When you regularly pause to recharge, you lower your risk of emotional exhaustion and compassion fatigue.

Enhances patience and emotional resilience: You're less likely to become irritable or overwhelmed when you've had space to rest and reset.

Sets a healthy example: You model resilience and balance for your loved one and others around you.

Practical Everyday Self-Care Strategies

These are realistic, low-cost self-care ideas that can fit into almost any caregiver's routine.

1.   Micro-breaks (5–15 minutes)

Step outside and feel the sun on your face.   Sip tea or coffee in silence.

Close your eyes and take 10 deep breaths.   Do gentle neck and shoulder stretches.

Listen to a favorite song or uplifting podcast episode.

2.   Daily "Me-Time" Rituals

Wake up 30 minutes earlier for quiet journaling or meditation.

Use aromatherapy in your caregiving space (lavender, eucalyptus, or citrus oils).

End your day with a warm bath or soothing music. Write one thing you're grateful for each night.

3.   Nutrition and Movement

Keep healthy snacks on hand (nuts, fruit, protein bars). Meal-prep simple, nourishing meals on Sundays.

Take short walks or do 10 minutes of movement (yoga, dancing, stretching).

4.   Emotional Check-ins

Call or text a supportive friend just to talk about you.

Use a self-care journal to track your feelings and needs. See a counselor or join a caregiver support group.

5.   Say "No" Without Guilt

You do not have to attend every family event or volunteer for every task. Set boundaries with extended family or visitors.

Allow yourself to rest without explaining or apologizing.

Grand (But Worthwhile) Self-Care Ideas

When the opportunity allows, these higher-level self-care actions can provide deep restoration.

1. *Respite Care*

Hire professional help for a weekend or a few hours a week. Ask a family member to take over care for a short period.

Apply for free or low-cost respite programs in your area.

2. *Therapeutic Getaways*

Book a weekend stay at a nearby hotel or retreat center.

Try a wellness-focused experience: yoga retreats, silent meditation weekends, or spa days.

3. *Creative Expression*

Start painting, gardening, writing, or crafting—anything that taps into your creative spirit.

Consider publishing your caregiving story or blog to help others.

4. *Invest in Professional Help*

Hire a life coach, therapist, or wellness expert who specializes in caregiver support. Take online courses or attend workshops on resilience, self-care, or grief processing.

Affirmations for the Caregiver's Soul

Sometimes we just need permission to prioritize ourselves. Let these words guide you:

"I matter, too."

"My needs are not a burden."

"Taking care of myself is an act of love." "Rest is not weakness—it is wisdom."

Reflection Exercise

Take a moment now to reflect:

What's one small self-care habit I can start today?

What's one boundary I need to protect my energy? When was the last time I did something just for me?

Write your answers in a journal or notebook. Revisit them weekly.

Being a caregiver is an honor, but it's also hard. You give so much of your heart, time, and energy. But you deserve care, too. When you make self-care a non-negotiable part of your routine, you not only preserve your well-being—you enhance your ability to love and support your loved one with strength and joy.

So go ahead—light the candle, make the tea, take the nap, call the friend. You're not stepping away from caregiving; you're stepping into your power as a whole, healthy, radiant human being.

In the following pages, you'll find helpful checklists designed to support you in your daily caregiving journey. These are suggested tools to help you stay organized and reduce overwhelm. Every caregiving situation is unique, so feel free to tailor these lists to match the specific needs of your loved one and your own routine. You are the expert on your caregiving experience—use these checklists as a flexible guide, not a rigid rulebook.

Caregiver Daily Checklist Care Tasks:

- Check on loved one's comfort & safety

- Administer medications (if applicable)

- Assist with meals / hydration

- Monitor mood & emotional well-being

- Assist with hygiene / mobility needs

- Record any changes in health

Notes:

Notes:

CONCLUSION

When I first stepped into the world of caregiving, I didn't have all the answers — not even close. I didn't have a guidebook or a roadmap. I learned through trial and error, through sleepless nights and quiet tears, through moments of doubt and glimpses of courage. Looking back, I often wonder how much easier some of those days might have been if I had someone walking alongside me — someone who understood, someone who could say, "I've been there, too." That's why I wrote this book. Not because I have it all figured out — but because I've lived it. I've walked this road. I know the weight of it, and I know the beauty of it, too.

I know what it feels like to try to do it all — to pour from an empty cup, to hide your exhaustion behind a brave face, to believe that asking for help is somehow weakness. I know what it's like to lose pieces of yourself along the way and wonder if you'll ever feel like you again.

But I also know this: You can thrive as a caregiver. You can care for your loved one and still care for yourself. You can dream new dreams. You can laugh again, breathe again, and live fully — right here in the middle of it all.

 If there is one thing I hope you carry with you from these pages, it's this: You are not alone. You are seen. You are stronger than you know. And you are doing an amazing job — even on the hard days.

So take a deep breath, dear friend. Give yourself grace. Ask for help when you need it. Protect your joy fiercely. And never forget — you are writing a story of love, courage, and resilience every single day.

You've got this — and I'm cheering you on every step of the way. With all my heart,

Edna

www.ingramcontent.com/pod-product-compliance
Lightning Source LLC
Chambersburg PA
CBHW070042110426
42741CB00036B/3232